I Can Make

PUPPETS

written and photographed by

Mary Wallace

Owl

Greey de Pencier Books

I Can Make Puppets

Books from OWL are published by Greey de Pencier Books,
179 John Street, Suite 500, Toronto, Ontario M5T 3G5

OWL and the OWL colophon are trademarks of the Young Naturalist Foundation.
Greey de Pencier is a licensed user of trademarks of the Young Naturalist Foundation.

Published simultaneously in the United States by Firefly Books (U.S.) Inc.,
P. O. Box 1338, Ellicott Station, Buffalo, NY 14205.

This book was published with the generous support of the Canada Council,
the Ontario Arts Council and the Government of Ontario through
the Ontario Publishing Centre.

Canadian Cataloguing in Publication Data

Wallace, Mary, 1950–
I can make puppets

ISBN 1-895688-24-8 (bound) ISBN 1-895688-20-5 (pbk)

1. Puppet making - Juvenile literature. I. Title

TT174.7.W35 1994   j745.592'24   C94-930473-5

Design & Art Direction: Julia Naimska
Cover photo, center: Ray Boudreau

Puppets on the front cover, counterclockwise from upper left:
String King, Mouthy Miniature, Prancing Pony, Finger Friends,
Silly Dragon, Best Buddy.

Other books by Mary Wallace
I Can Make Toys
How to Make Great Stuff to Wear
How to Make Great Stuff for Your Room

Printed in Hong Kong

A   B   C   D   E   F

CONTENTS

LET'S MAKE PUPPETS

You can make all the puppets in this book. It's easy. It's fun. These two pages show the things used to make puppets in this book, but you can use other things if you like. You'll find most of what you'll need around the house — remember to get permission to use what you find.

- ribbon
- white glue
- tape
- markers
- pencils
- hole punch
- felt
- button

- sock
- stocking
- aluminum foil
- star stickers
- paint stir stick
- large safety pins
- rubber bands
- yarn
- mittens
- face paint

- paper towels
- sponges
- paper tubes
- cardboard box
- newspaper
- Bristol board
- stapler
- construction paper
- acrylic/fabric paint

- colored paper
- tissue paper
- string
- paper fasteners
- needle and thread
- googly eyes
- scissors
- bottle tops

- footed sleepers
- towel
- small scarf
- face cloth
- T-shirt
- stretchy pants
- polyester stuffing

PUPPET PLAY

Get to Know your Puppet

Every puppet is special. You can give your puppets faces that show how they feel. And when you make them talk and move, they will really come alive!

1. GET YOUR PUPPETS TO TELL ABOUT THEMSELVES

- names
- what they do every day
- favorite things, places, games
- what they like to eat and drink

I like purple pickles and pineapple punch. Let's go out for a picnic lunch!

Hi! I'm Rosie and I love to sing and dance.

2. TWO PUPPETS CAN TALK TO EACH OTHER IN DIFFERENT VOICES

- happy
- angry
- sad
- surprised
- silly
- excited
- scared

Please don't wave your wand and make my treasure disappear!

OK. But only if you'll breathe fire so we can toast marshmallows.

See us run and jump!

3. MAKE YOUR PUPPET MOVE

- bow
- kiss
- twist
- fall
- shake hands
- sleep
- pick things up
- put things down
- move things
- walk
- jump
- run
- chase
- dance
- push
- pull
- nod
- shake
- cry
- laugh

These are some of the ways you can play with your puppets. But we know you can think of more. When you get to know your puppets, there are lots of amazing things they can say and do. Have fun!

SILLY DRAGON

- *grown-up to help sew*
- Bristol board
- scissors
- white glue
- an old sock
- crumpled newspaper
- 2 rubber bands
- felt
- googly eyes
- needle and thread

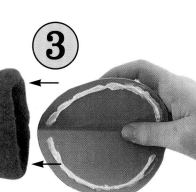

①

fold

cut circle
from Bristol board
and fold in half

②

apply
glue

③

push circle into
sock

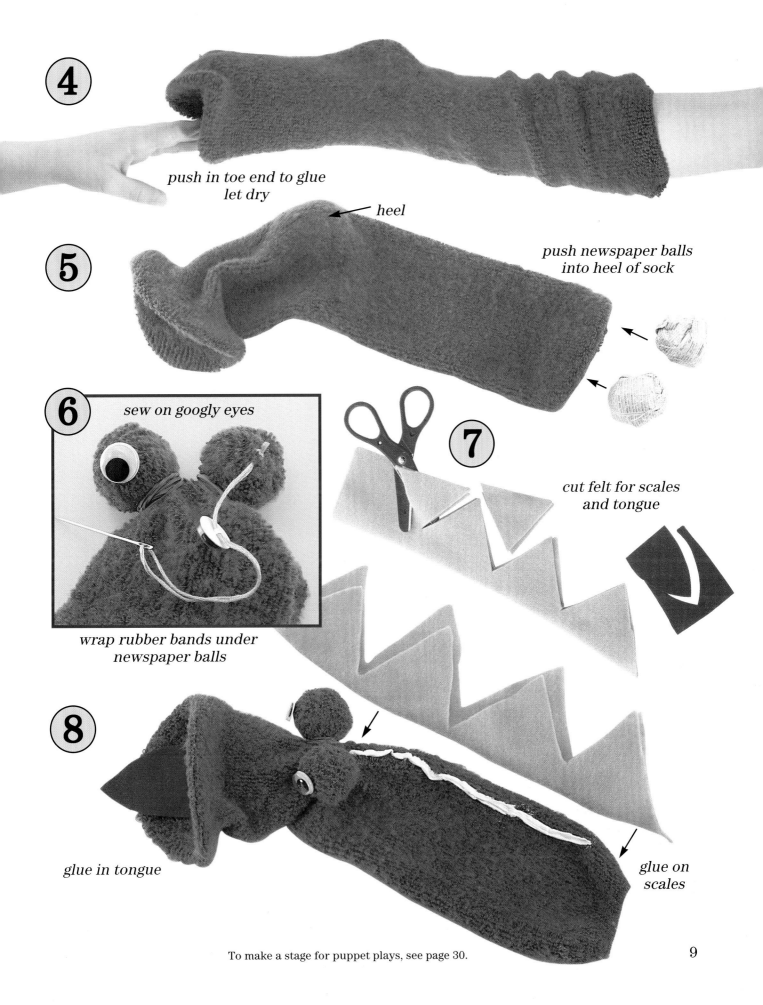

4 push in toe end to glue
let dry

heel

5 push newspaper balls
into heel of sock

6 sew on googly eyes

wrap rubber bands under
newspaper balls

7 cut felt for scales
and tongue

8 glue in tongue

glue on
scales

To make a stage for puppet plays, see page 30.

MOUTHY MINIATURES

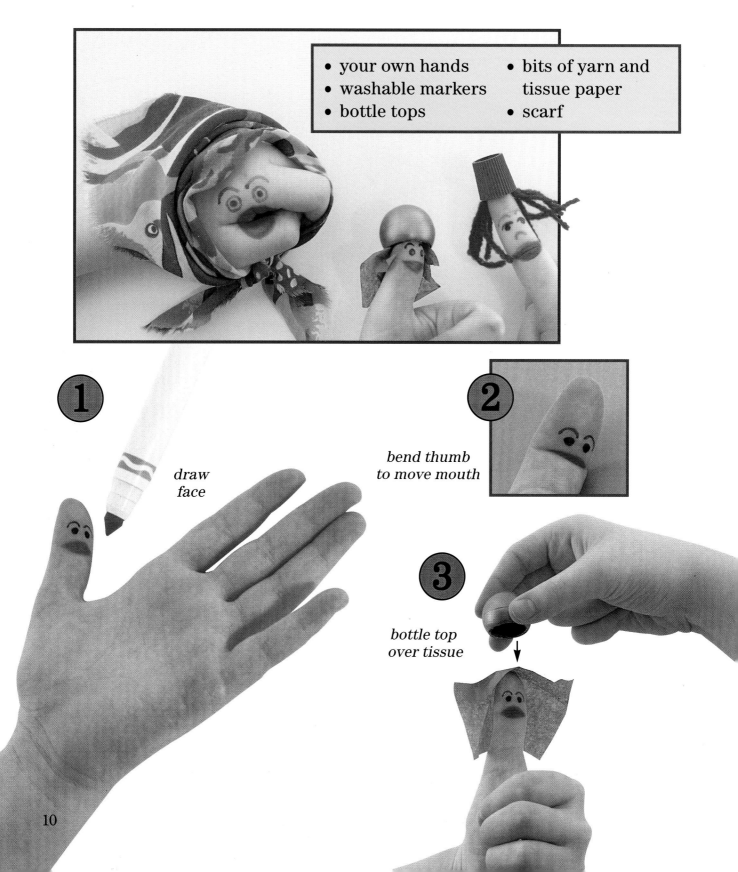

- your own hands
- washable markers
- bottle tops
- bits of yarn and tissue paper
- scarf

1 draw face

2 bend thumb to move mouth

3 bottle top over tissue

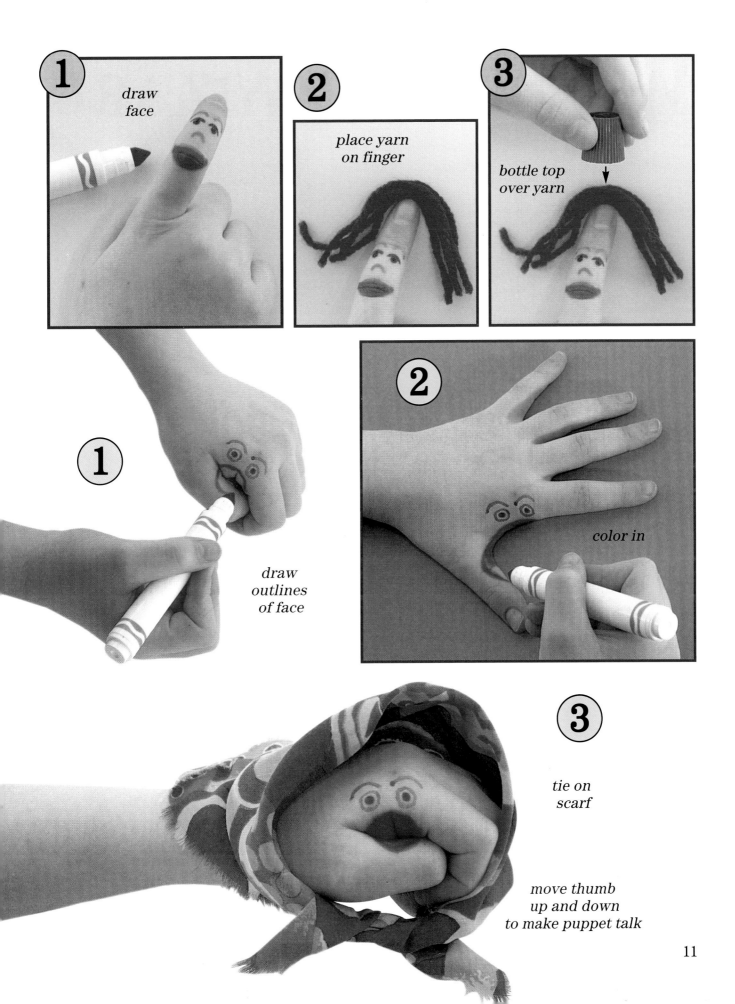

1 draw face

2 place yarn on finger

3 bottle top over yarn

1 draw outlines of face

2 color in

3 tie on scarf

move thumb up and down to make puppet talk

WONDERFUL WIZARD

- small paper tube
- scissors
- paper towel
- white glue
- water
- soupspoon
- plastic container
- markers or colored tape
- Bristol board
- tape
- face cloth
- star stickers
- *decorate as you like*

1 *cut piece of tube*

2 *tear paper towel into pieces*

3 *mix 3 soupspoons of glue and 3 soupspoons of water*

cover table

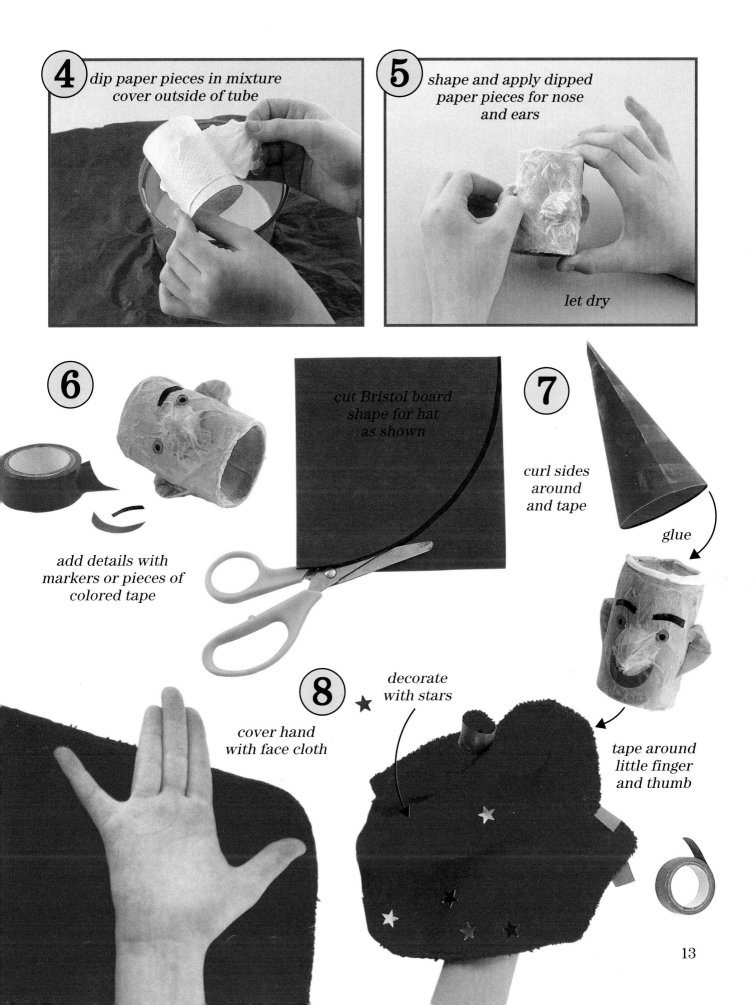

4 dip paper pieces in mixture cover outside of tube

5 shape and apply dipped paper pieces for nose and ears

let dry

6 add details with markers or pieces of colored tape

cut Bristol board shape for hat as shown

7 curl sides around and tape

glue

8 cover hand with face cloth

decorate with stars

tape around little finger and thumb

13

PINK PIG

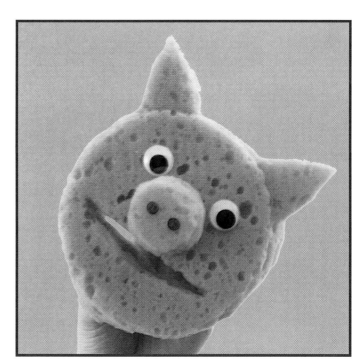

- 2 soft sponges
- marker
- scissors
- white glue
- 2 googly eyes
- fabric paint
- *decorate as you like*

1 *draw three lines like this on sponge*

cut short lines part way through

2

3 *cut long line all the way through*

4 *try on and adjust cuts*

5 trim off corners

6 cut ears and nose from other sponge

7 glue on

8 paint details let dry

CHIN CHUCKLER

- your own chin
- washable markers or face paint
- rubber band for long hair
- light-weight scarf or T-shirt
- bed
- *decorate as you like*

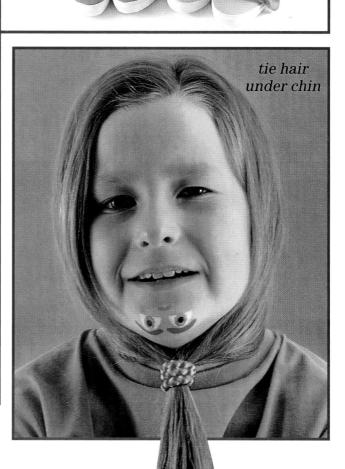

1 *make your chin into an upside-down face*

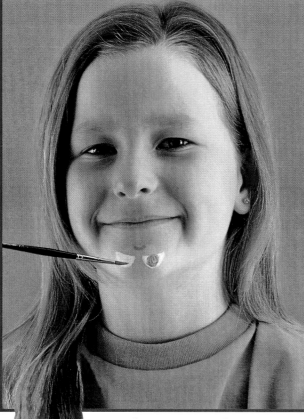

draw eyes and nose

tie hair under chin

2 *cover the top half of your face using T-shirt or scarf*

pull on T-shirt upside-down

wrap scarf loosely and tie in back

3

lie with your head hanging over side of bed and make funny faces for your friends

FINGER FRIENDS

- colored construction paper
- scissors
- white glue
- markers
- tape
- *decorate as you like*

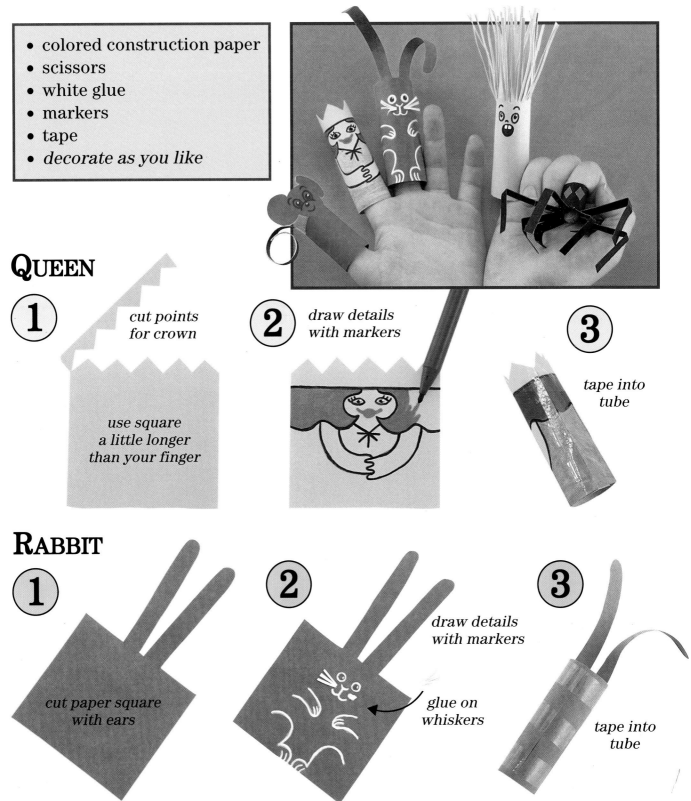

QUEEN

1 cut points for crown

use square
a little longer
than your finger

2 draw details
with markers

3 tape into
tube

RABBIT

1 cut paper square
with ears

2 draw details
with markers

glue on
whiskers

3 tape into
tube

MOUSE

1 cut out shape for head

use square a little longer than your finger

2 draw details with markers

3 tape into tube add paper tail

MISS MUFFET

1 cut half-way down to make hair

use rectangle about twice as long as your finger

2 draw details with markers

3 tape into tube

SPIDER

1 use rectangle a little longer than your finger

cut 8 legs leaving strip on top for ring

2 tape ring

3 glue on paper eyes

bend legs

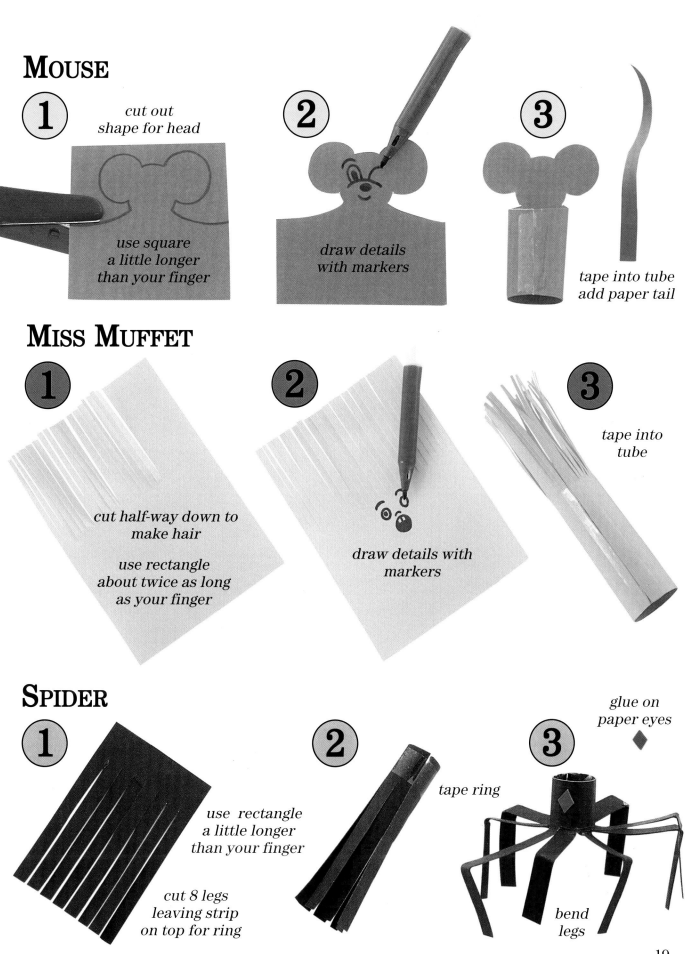

BEST BUDDY

- *grown-up to help with sewing*
- cardboard box
- scissors
- an old pair of stretchy pants
- 2 rubber bands
- polyester stuffing
- ribbon
- googly eyes
- footed sleepers
- needle and thread
- mittens

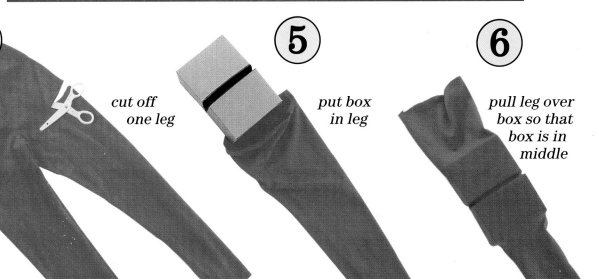

① cut through box on three sides

② bend open along fourth side to make mouth

③ try on mouth and adjust

④ cut off one leg

⑤ put box in leg

⑥ pull leg over box so that box is in middle

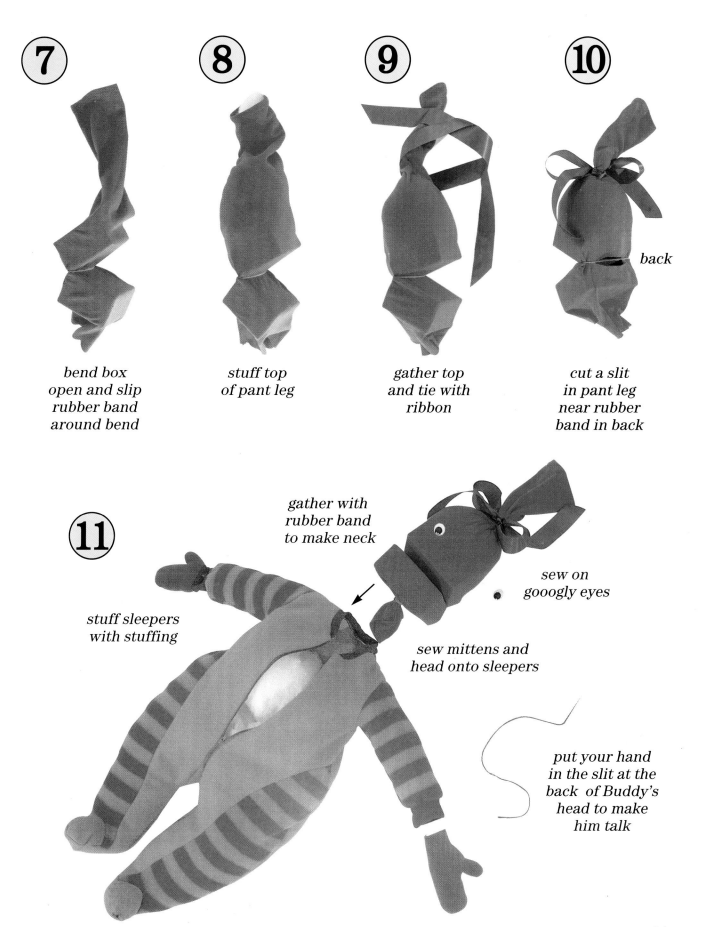

7 bend box open and slip rubber band around bend

8 stuff top of pant leg

9 gather top and tie with ribbon

10 cut a slit in pant leg near rubber band in back

back

11

gather with rubber band to make neck

sew on gooogly eyes

stuff sleepers with stuffing

sew mittens and head onto sleepers

put your hand in the slit at the back of Buddy's head to make him talk

ROSIE ROCK STAR

- *grown-up to help with stapling*
- paint stir stick
- toilet paper tube
- stocking
- scissors
- 2 rubber bands
- felt
- stapler
- markers
- yarn
- glue
- *decorate as you like*

(1) cut foot off stocking

slide tube onto stick

(2) pull stocking leg over tube

(3) secure stocking ends to stick with rubber bands

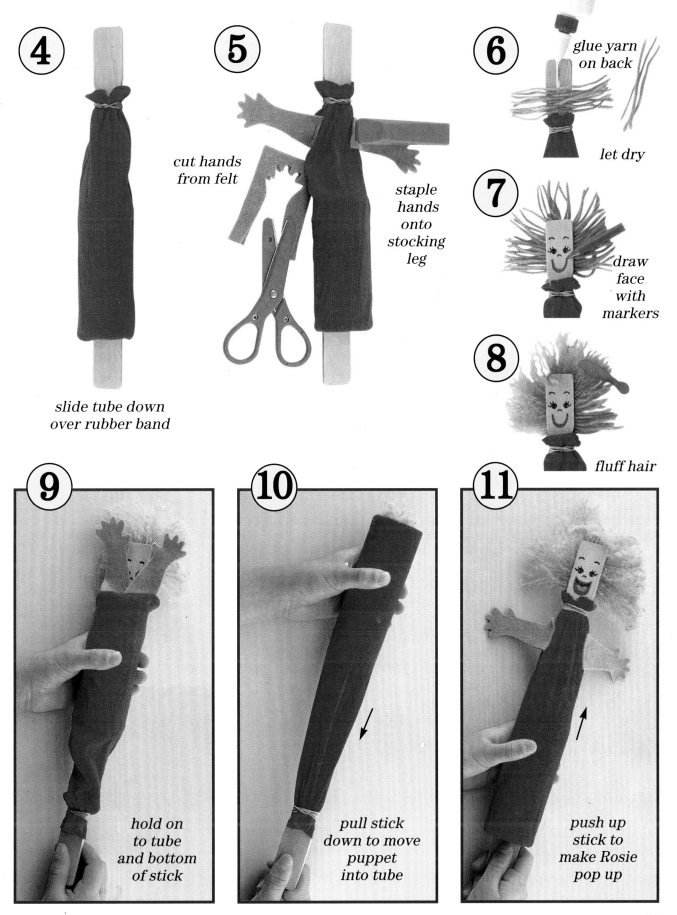

4 slide tube down over rubber band

5 cut hands from felt

staple hands onto stocking leg

6 glue yarn on back

let dry

7 draw face with markers

8 fluff hair

9 hold on to tube and bottom of stick

10 pull stick down to move puppet into tube

11 push up stick to make Rosie pop up

23

FINGER WIGGLERS

- Bristol board
- pencil
- scissors
- tape
- markers
- button
- *decorate as you like*

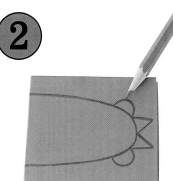

GABBY GATOR

1 *fold*

draw outline

2 *add nostrils and teeth*

3 *cut out shape*

snip off bottom nostrils

4 *cut strips for finger rings include eye bumps on one*

5 *tape strips into rings*

6 *tape rings to outside of head*

fold nostrils and eyes up

fold teeth in

TWEETER

① *fold and glue*

②

③

cut out bird
and beak

cut strips
for finger rings

tape rings to
back of wings

move fingers in and
out to flap wings

ELEPHANT

①

②

③ have a grown-up
help you start the holes

draw outline on
Bristol board

trace button for holes

draw details with markers

SUNSHINE

①

cut body
from
Bristol
board

draw
details
with
markers

fold
feet up

②

cut strips for
finger rings

tape into rings

③

tape rings
to back
of legs

STRING KING

- scissors
- felt
- Bristol board
- markers
- toilet paper tube
- hole punch
- 6 paper fasteners
- string
- paper towel tube
- aluminum foil
- *decorate as you like*

1

cut arms, legs and cape from felt

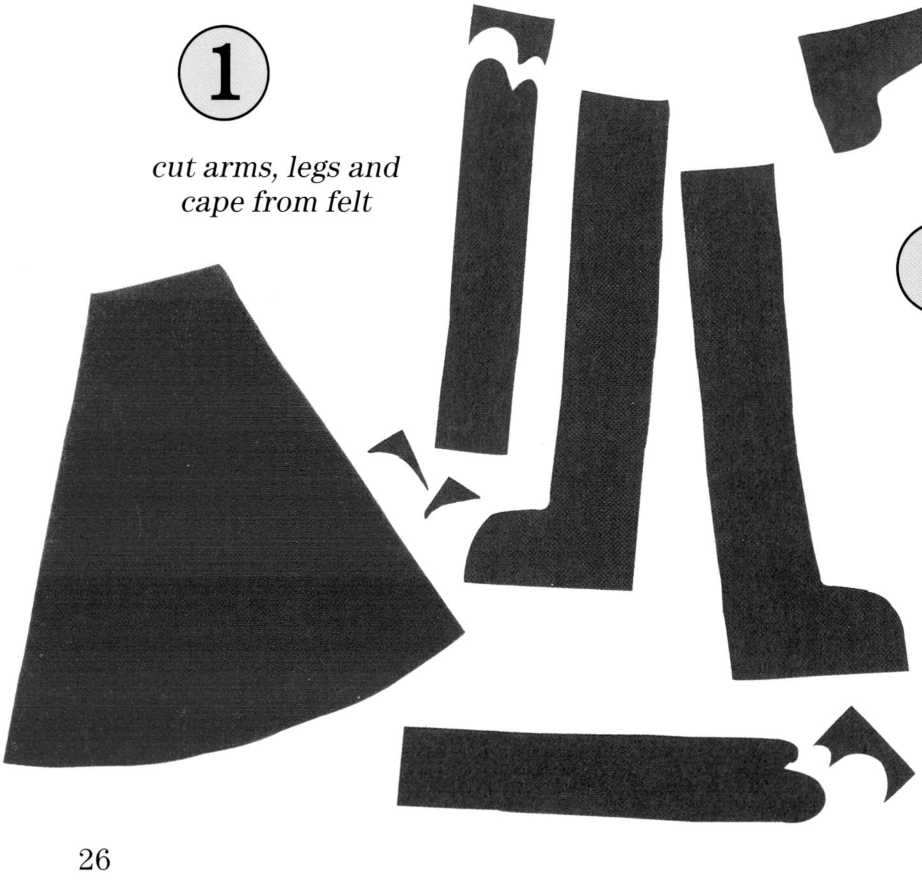

2 *cut head from Bristol board*

draw details with markers

3 punch holes as shown

punch 6 holes in tube as shown

4 push paper fasteners through from inside of tube

attach arms and legs to tube

5 attach head and cape

6 loop and tie strings around long tube

tie string to ends of arms and top of crown

decorate

To make a horse for your king to ride, see page 28.

PRANCING PONY

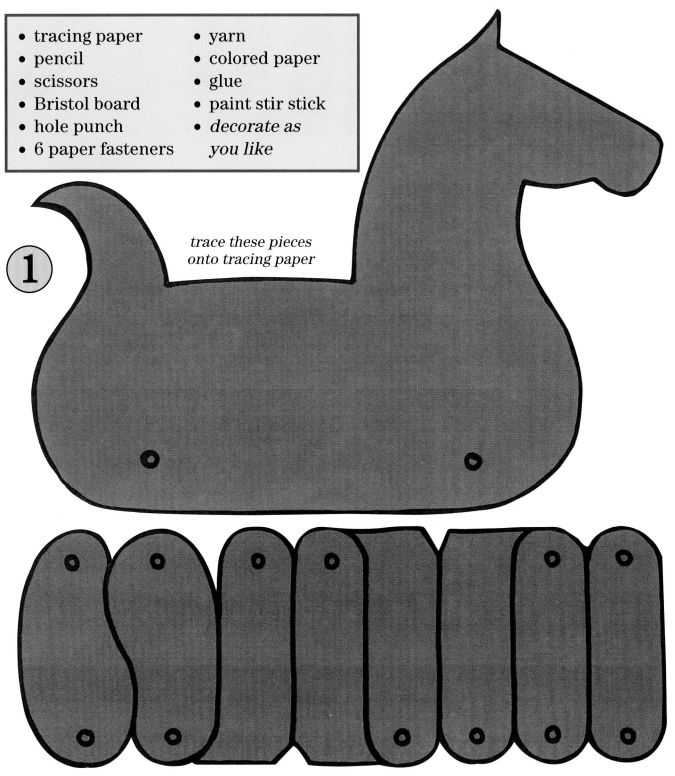

- tracing paper
- pencil
- scissors
- Bristol board
- hole punch
- 6 paper fasteners
- yarn
- colored paper
- glue
- paint stir stick
- *decorate as you like*

①

trace these pieces onto tracing paper

2 back leg tops   *4 lower legs*   *2 front leg tops*

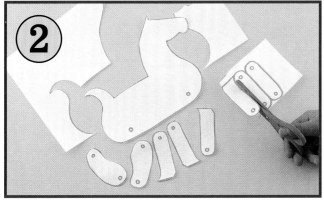

cut out pieces

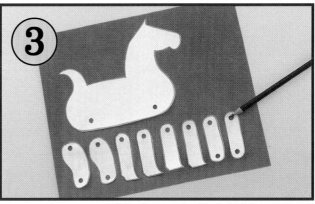

trace shapes and holes onto Bristol board

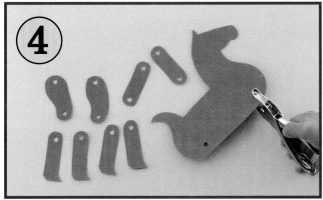

cut out and punch holes

**bend
fastener
ends
loosely**

2 paper fasteners attach leg tops to body

4 paper fasteners attach lower legs to tops

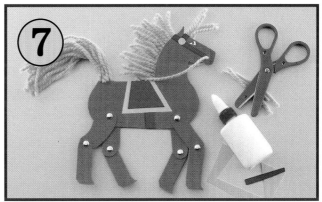

cut and glue paper and yarn details

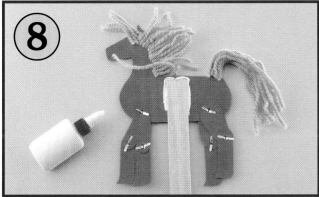

glue stick on back and let dry

jiggle to make pony prance

To make a stage for puppet plays, see page 30.

PUPPET STAGE

- *grown-up to help with pins*
- 2 chairs
- 4 large towels
- broomstick
- 2 large safety pins
- construction paper
- tape
- markers
- *decorate as you like*

1 *push seats of chairs together*

2

drape chairs with towels

3 *balance broomstick on chair backs*

use safety pins to secure towel

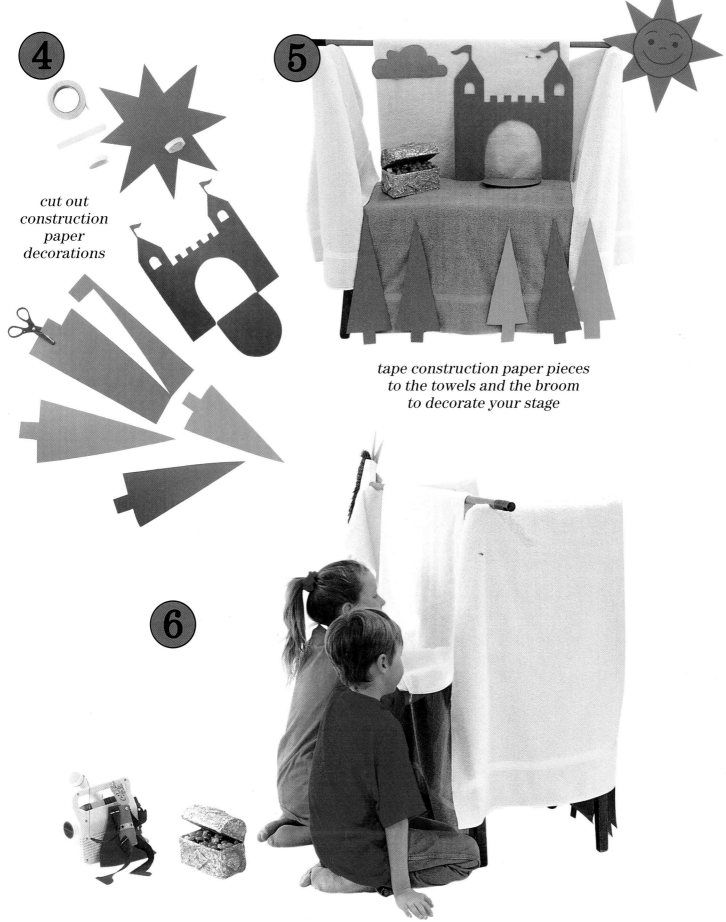

4

*cut out
construction
paper
decorations*

5

*tape construction paper pieces
to the towels and the broom
to decorate your stage*

6

To see how to put on a puppet play, turn the page! 31

PUTTING ON A PUPPET PLAY

- make puppets talk to each other or the audience
- only one puppet speaks at a time
- move only the puppet that is speaking
- hold the puppet so the audience can see its face
- act out a fairy tale or tell a story